SELENA

A Real-Life Reader Biography

Barbara Marvis

Mitchell Lane Publishers, Inc.

P.O. Box 200 • Childs, Maryland 21916

Mitchell Lane
PUBLISHERS

Third Printing
Real-Life Reader Biographies

Selena	Robert Rodriguez	Mariah Carey	Rafael Palmeiro
Tommy Nuñez	Trent Dimas	Cristina Saralegui	Andres Galarraga
Oscar De La Hoya	Gloria Estefan	Jimmy Smits	Mary Joe Fernandez
Cesar Chavez	Sinbad	Paula Abdul	Vanessa Williams
Chuck Norris	Celine Dion	Mia Hamm	LeAnn Rimes

Library of Congress Cataloging-in-Publication Data
Marvis, Barbara J.
    Selena / Barbara Marvis.
        p. cm. — (A real-life reader biography)
    Includes index.
    Summary: Relates the story of the rise to fame and the tragic death of this Texas-born Tejano singer.
    ISBN 1-883845-47-5 (library)
    1. Selena, 1971-1995—Juvenile literature. 2. Tejano musicians—Biography—Juvenile literature. [1. Selena, 1971-1995. 2. Singers. 3. Tejano music. 4. Women—Biography. 5. Mexican Americans—Biography.] I. Title. II. Series.
ML3930.S43M37 1997
782.42164—dc21
[B]   97-21960
                                                                                                       CIP
                                                                                                  AC MN

ABOUT THE AUTHOR: Barbara Marvis has been a writer for twenty years. She is the author of several books for young adults including the *Contemporary American Success Stories* series and *Tommy Nuñez: NBA Referee/Taking My Best Shot*. She holds a B.S. degree in English and communications from West Chester State University and an M.Ed. in remedial reading from the University of Delaware. She specializes in writing books for children that can be read on several reading levels. She lives with her husband, Bob, and their five children in northern Maryland.

PHOTO CREDITS: cover: AP Photo/George Gongora-Corpus Christi Caller-Times; p. 4 sketch by Barbara Tidman; p. 6 courtesy Q Productions; p. 11 AP/Wide World Photos; p. 12 courtesy EMI Records; p. 14 Bettmann; p. 16 Reuters/Archive Photos; p. 19 AP/Wide World Photos; p. 23 Reuters/Archive Photos

ACKNOWLEDGMENTS: The following story has been thoroughly researched and checked for accuracy. To the best of our knowledge, it represents a true story. Though we attempted to contact each person profiled in our Real-Life Reader Biographies, for various reasons, we are unable to authorize every story. Our sincerest appreciation goes to Joe Villarreal at Q Productions and Sandy Friedman of Rogers & Cowan for the information about Selena on which this story is based.

Table of Contents

Chapter 1
Young Selena

Selena Quintanilla was born in Lake Jackson, Texas, on April 16, 1971. She was the youngest of three children. She had an older brother, Abraham III, who is called A.B. She also had an older sister named Suzette. Marcela and Abraham Quintanilla, Jr. are their parents.

Selena grew up in Texas.

The Quintanilla family has lived and worked in Texas for more than one hundred years. Selena's great grandparents had come to the United States from Mexico.

Selena's father loved music. When he was young, he belonged to a band. He wanted his children to love music, too. When Selena was just five years old, Abraham began to teach the children about music. They formed a little band called *Selena y Los Dinos* (Selena and

Young Selena loved school. She had a perky personality and was well liked.

the boys). A.B. played bass. Suzette played the drums, and Selena sang. They played at weddings and parties.

Selena went to first grade at Oran M. Roberts Elementary School. She had many friends. She was happy and she loved going to school. The students at her school were from all over Latin America. Their parents had come to Texas through a special program to work at Dow Chemical. Selena's father worked as a shipping clerk for Dow Chemical, too.

When Selena was nine, her father quit his job at Dow Chemical to start his own restaurant. Everyone in the family had to help. On weekends, their band performed at the restaurant. Though they worked very hard, the restaurant failed. In Texas, times were tough because the

When Selena was nine, her father started his own restaurant. Their band played on weekends.

oil industry was not doing well. People had no money to go out to eat. The Quintanillas could not keep their restaurant. They lost their house and most of their belongings. They had to move.

Abraham decided the family should earn a living making music. They moved to Corpus Christi, Texas, but they spent most of their time in a battered van, traveling the back country of south Texas. They played at dances, weddings, and festivals. Sometimes, only ten people would come to hear them play. It was hard to make a living that way. They did not make much money. They ate a lot of hamburgers, and they shared everything.

Chapter 2
Early Career

Selena's father made the decisions for the band. He wanted the band to play Tejano music, which is sung in Spanish. But Selena did not know how to speak Spanish. She grew up speaking only English. Her father taught her Spanish music. This is how Selena learned to speak Spanish.

Selena went to West Oso Junior High School in Corpus Christi. She was very good in school. She had to stop going when she was in eighth

When Selena was young, she did not know how to speak Spanish.

grade because she traveled so much with her family. She missed too many days. She took home–school courses instead.

In 1985, Selena made her first real recording for a local record label called Manny Guerra. She was just fourteen years old.

When the Quintanillas were on the road, they met Johnny Canales, who was another traveling bandsman. Abraham had known Johnny in high school, when they both had had bands. Later, Canales hosted a Spanish-language television show. Selena appeared on his show many times. She was always a big hit.

Selena wanted everyone to like her music. She loved to sing for people. She enjoyed entertaining them. This is what made her happy.

Selena wanted everyone to like her music.

Chapter 3
Stardom

Selena wanted everyone to like her music. This was not easy. She was part of the Tejano culture. Tejanos are Mexican-Americans who are born or live in Texas. Some people do not like them. Young Tejanos speak and read English. The Mexicans say they do not speak Spanish correctly. The Anglo-Texans say their English is not good.

In 1989, Selena met Chris Perez. He had joined Selena's band to play guitar. In 1991, they began to date.

Selena met Chris Perez in 1989. They were married in 1992.

Selena was known as a good girl, but she wore heavy makeup and skin-tight clothes when she performed.

They were married in 1992. Selena and her band became more and more well known.

In 1989, the band signed a big record deal with EMI Latin. They recorded six albums. Each album was more popular than the one before. Selena was a millionaire by the time she was nineteen. By the time she was twenty-one, thousands of people came to her concerts to hear her sing. Then, to top it off, the album *Selena Live!* won a Grammy in 1994 for the best Mexican-American performance.

In late 1994, Selena signed a record deal with SBK records (a division of EMI) to record an English-language album. The album was to be released in mid-1995.

Soon, people wanted a Selena fan club. Yolanda Saldívar called Selena's father, Abraham, to ask if she could start a fan club for Selena.

Selena was a millionaire by the time she was nineteen.

Yolanda Saldívar was a nurse from San Antonio. She wanted to work with Selena. She had no children of her own. She treated Selena as if she were very special. But there were two sides to Yolanda. Some people thought she was devoted to Selena. Other people thought she was very mean.

Chapter 4
Yolanda Saldívar

At first, Abraham did not call Yolanda back. Then the family discussed the fan club. Finally, they thought it might be a good idea.

Yolanda Saldívar was a nurse from San Antonio, Texas. She liked Selena. She wanted to help the singer become more popular. The Quintanillas decided to hire her to manage the fan club. For the first two years, Yolanda did very well.

Selena thought she would reward Yolanda for being so good to her.

Yolanda Saldívar was hired to run Selena's fan club.

She put her in charge of her new shop, Selena Etc., where she sold clothes and jewelry. But Yolanda did not get along with the other people who worked in the store.

Many people said Yolanda was mean to them. They said she protected Selena and did not let anyone talk to her. Then they said Yolanda was taking money that belonged to Selena and using it to buy things for herself. Because Selena liked Yolanda, she did not tell her what everyone was saying.

For Christmas 1994, Selena's employees put their money together to buy Selena a present. They had a ring made especially for her. Yolanda told Selena that the ring was from just her. She did not tell Selena that the ring was from her other friends, too. Yolanda kept the money that Selena's employees

Many people said Yolanda was mean to them.

had given for the ring. Then she paid for the ring with Selena's credit card.

People said Yolanda was taking the fan club money.

Soon, Abraham began hearing of problems with the fan club. Some fans said they had sent money for a photograph, T-shirt, and CD. But they had not received anything. People said Yolanda was taking the fan club money. Yolanda said it wasn't true.

The family wanted to ask Yolanda about the missing money. In January 1995, Abraham spoke to her. She said she had done nothing wrong. More money was missing from the shop. In early March, the family spoke to Yolanda again. She said that some people were lying about her. They wanted to make her look bad.

Chapter 5
Tragedy

On March 13, 1995, Yolanda bought a gun. Then she went to Mexico and took some of Selena's papers with her. Selena called her and told her to bring the papers back.

On March 30, Yolanda called Selena to tell her that she had brought her papers. She would meet with Selena if she would come to her hotel room alone. But Selena went with her husband, Chris. Yolanda was angry that Selena had

On March 13, 1995, Yolanda bought a gun.

brought him along. She would not give them all the papers. She told Selena to come back the next day.

On March 31, 1995, Selena went to see Yolanda alone. They had an argument. Selena told Yolanda she was fired. Then she turned to leave.

Yolanda took out her gun and shot Selena in the back. Selena stumbled to the motel office.

Yolanda shot Selena in the back. Selena died the same day.

An ambulance came to take Selena to the hospital. She died later that day.

On April 3, 1995, Selena was buried. More than 30,000 people walked by her casket. Thousands of people had loved Selena.

Just days after her death, the movie *Don Juan DeMarco* opened. Selena had a small part in the movie. Someday, she might have been a movie star.

When she died, Selena had been in the middle of making her first English-language album. Although it was unfinished, her album *Dreaming of You* was released soon after her death.

In March 1997, the movie *Selena* was released. The Quintanilla family helped with the movie.

When Selena was alive, she used to speak to schoolchildren. Many young girls thought of her as a big sister. They loved to hear her sing. Now, she sings with the angels.

Now Selena can only sing with the angels.

More than 30,000 people attended Selena's funeral.

Chronology

- Born April 16, 1971, in Lake Jackson, Texas; mother: Marcela; father: Abraham Quintanilla
- At age nine, began singing with the family band
- Moved to Corpus Christi, Texas, after father's restaurant failed
- Learned to speak Spanish so that she could sing Tejano music
- Attended West Oso Junior High School
- Left school after eighth grade to travel with the band; took home–school courses
- 1985, made first recording for a local label
- 1987, won Tejano Music Award for female vocalist and best performer of the year
- 1989, signed with EMI Latin
- 1992, married Chris Perez
- 1994, *Selena Live!* won a Grammy
- March 31, 1995, shot and killed by Yolanda Saldívar

Index